A Year Full of Grace

Lisa Marie

WESTBOW
PRESS®
A DIVISION OF THOMAS NELSON
& ZONDERVAN

This book is a work of non-fiction. Unless otherwise noted, the author
and the publisher make no explicit guarantees as to the accuracy of
the information contained in this book and in some cases, names
of people and places have been altered to protect their privacy.

Scripture taken from the King James Version of the Bible.

WestBow Press books may be ordered through booksellers or by contacting:

WestBow Press
A Division of Thomas Nelson & Zondervan
1663 Liberty Drive
Bloomington, IN 47403
www.westbowpress.com
1 (866) 928-1240

Because of the dynamic nature of the Internet, any web addresses or
links contained in this book may have changed since publication and
may no longer be valid. The views expressed in this work are solely those
of the author and do not necessarily reflect the views of the publisher,
and the publisher hereby disclaims any responsibility for them.

Any people depicted in stock imagery provided by Thinkstock are
models, and such images are being used for illustrative purposes only.
Certain stock imagery © Thinkstock.

ISBN: 978-1-5127-6643-1 (sc)
ISBN: 978-1-5127-6642-4 (hc)
ISBN: 978-1-5127-6644-8 (e)

Library of Congress Control Number: 2016919453

Print information available on the last page.

WestBow Press rev. date: 12/01/2016

Contents

Pleasant Valley Presbyterian Church, Miller SD

L. Hume Ward was called as pastor, and assumed his duties April 15, 1950. During the Pastorate of Rev. Ward, Pleasant Valley Presbyterian Church was organized in the Southern part of Hand County. Jack Johnson, Miller did much of the interior woodwork on this beautiful church. The day it opened there were numerous baptisms. When the church closed in the 1980's it was still being used as a community center for many events. 4-H meetings were held in the basement as well as card parties, wedding and baby showers. General elections were also held there. Photo courtesy of Christian Begeman of Prairie Sanctuaries.

This book is dedicated to Jim - one of the most Grace Full men I have ever met.

Prologue

For by grace are ye saved through faith; and that not of yourselves: it is the gift of God: Not of works, lest any man should boast. For we are his workmanship, created in Christ Jesus unto good works, which God hath before ordained that we should walk in them.

—Ephesians 2:8–10

Pursuing God's grace can take nearly a lifetime, and sometimes we do not know where or when it will begin to appear to us. The first two quarters of my life had been consumed with a quest for peace, happiness, but more importantly, God's grace. What I didn't realize until most recently is that all three of these were always well within my grasp, much closer than I ever realized. I was given the same opportunities, and I possessed some of the same qualities as many of my peers. Did I finish at the top of my graduating class? No. However, I did graduate with honors, but I chose not to further my education through books and school at that young age and just get on with life, learning most of what I knew through the school of hard knocks. Marrying at age eighteen and starting a family soon after, left little room for self-indulgences on my part.

My life experiences from then on taught me a great deal; however, the gnawing ache inside me to further my education never left my mind. When we do not live up to our potential, not only do we fall short of our own aptitudes and skills, we shortchange ourselves from the true feelings of inner peace, happiness, and grace that many times come to us when we finally achieve those goals we've set for ourselves. All of this, though, can get buried somewhere deep inside of us, and we choose to carry on with our lives, making the most of what we face right in front of us, as opposed to taking the road less traveled filled with a few detours and pitfalls.

I think I was very good at adapting to my surroundings and situations, but I always felt as though I was living way outside the parameters of my own abilities when it came to my intelligence, my love of people, my ability to show compassion for others, and the use of my own unique personality traits. I didn't know at the time that the grace God gave to me to begin to make positive changes in my life was always well within my soul, just waiting to be released.

This was a year of transformation, positive as well as not, where I began that journey to faith with my Lord. I was not always able to envision the grace bestowed on me, but as I kept changing and growing in my walk I realized it was not out of sight completely. Little by little, God gave me opportunities to see the immeasurable love that he has for all of us. He has shown me his grace in all of his works and I am anticipating what the next year holds for me and my life.

Better is a poor man who walks in his integrity,
than a rich man who is crooked in his ways.

Chapter 1

Graceful Living

January

And he said unto me, my grace is sufficient for thee: for my strength is made perfect in weakness. Most gladly therefore will I rather glory in my infirmities, that the power of Christ may rest upon me.

—2 Corinthians 12:9

Grace is most often referred to as God's free and unmerited gift to us, regardless of anything we might have done. You cannot build up good deeds in order to receive more grace than your neighbor does. Sometimes the pursuit of perfection can limit us from realizing that all humans receive God's forgiveness and grace, regardless of how well we are doing on this planet during our lifetime. God gives common grace in the form of the beauty of the earth, our ability to live and work, our love of family and friends, and the capability to learn and grow. The grace of forgiveness from God cannot be duplicated; all we can do is receive it. Rejecting His grace is one of the most common sins of man.

Grace in the Old Testament of the Bible meant kindness, well-favored, merciful, pleasant, and precious. Grace in the New Testament meant to benefit from God's mercy and the love and joy bestowed on His people in spite of what they deserve.

"Hail Mary, full of grace. The Lord is with Thee." Many Catholic believers today recite this passage from the Bible with little regard to its meaning. How much grace is that? Are we all full of grace from the Lord? The Bible says Mary was full of grace, but not without sin, from the moment of conception. Can we measure the amount that we receive? Are only a certain chosen few full of grace?

Nancy Reagan died March 7, 2016, and was best described as "a woman of grace." I believe some news reporters used this term in reference to the way she lived, as she possessed immeasurable self-control, spoke with impeccable manners, and seemed easy to get along with. She served as first lady with unbelievable power, class, and grace and left her mark on the world.[1] Other women throughout history are described as having had an abundance of grace, living a life of mercy toward their fellow humans, having compassion toward the helpless, or just possessing high esteem.

Why aren't men described as often as having grace? The grace of Jesus Christ says He has given all of us, men and women, His unending mercy and forgiveness. Some men surely possess a certain amount of grace, but they would be more than likely not to admit it or even recognize it. But is it ever written in a man's obituary that he led a spiritual life full of grace? I believe there are many men in this world right now living a fruitful life and

---

[1] See more at www.legacy.com/obituaries/tributes/obituary.

growing in the grace of God. There are also many women who would love to share this grace with the men in their life.

Many men I have met have subtle grace that goes unnoticed unless you attempt to look for it. In a man, grace is most recognized when he shows respect for others, remains calm in the face of disaster, and has unselfish love for his family and friends. "Growing old gracefully" is used to describe distinguished men in their later years. Some men just have that natural, younger look and come across as graceful in their attractive appearance. It generally is inherited but could be determined by the lifestyle they lead. Good health plays a part in how their skin looks, but how they look on the inside determines how gracefully they age and how younger people who know them admire them.

"Graceful" is very often used to refer to a dancer or performer who glides across the stage with the utmost ease. This sort of gracefulness has to be acquired and strived for. It doesn't come without hard work and discipline. Grace in a marriage could be given to each other, which would mean complete forgiveness and kindness toward the one we will spend the rest of our life with. Although many couples attempt to emulate God's grace in their own marriages, they often fall short because of their sinful natures.

Graciousness abides in a person's soul when he or she manages to forgive others easily, spreads kindness, is merciful to others, and welcomes others with courtesy. "Gracious" can also mean to have tact, good taste, and elegance. A warm welcome shown to one another exemplifies our graciousness.

For years, when I attended church on Sunday, our pastor would begin his sermon with these exact words, "Grace be to you and peace from God our Father and from the Lord Jesus Christ." These familiar words would settle me in my seat and help me turn off distracting thoughts that kept racing through my mind so I would be ready to absorb the words the minister was about to say. The church would grow quieter, and our gracious pastor would begin his message of the week by filling our minds with the Lord's word. That split second of silence before the sermon always helped me shut out the world and absorb more of what I needed to hear.

At this time I began thinking about this widely known word, "grace," and how many of us use it casually in speaking but rarely see its total significance in our lives. Growing in the grace of God should be one of our many Christian desires and goals as we move through our life on this earth.

Now that I have become more aware of the overuse of this word, I know that God's grace is all around me and nothing I can do in this lifetime will warrant any more merit, or grace, from God than anyone else has. God gives us this kind of grace without any stipulations or restrictions. Our acceptance of this perfect grace is God's one desire. Whether or not the people we encounter deserve our grace, God would like us to grant it to them anyway.

That is the real challenge we all face. If we look for grace in our own character and attempt to live it out in our personal lives, we are satisfying God's desires for us. Do you find yourself having difficulty bestowing grace onto others, especially the kind of unconditional grace that we receive from our heavenly Father?

Having incredible anxiety over everything unimaginable does not take away tomorrow's troubles. It just removes all of today's peace. Memories of the past can help us through a loss or breakup, but they can also keep us from truly enjoying the present. God intends for us to learn from our mistakes of the past but not to continue worrying forever about things we cannot change. The older I get, the more I realize the importance of the present time and how short our life is here on earth. When we strive to live our lives with courage and grace, we look more to the future in God's kingdom and less to the sorrow here on earth.

Our dreams can keep us locked in the past. After the ending of a thirty-plus-year marriage, I would have the most vivid dreams about my life, and they would bring me straight back to the time before it all stopped. After about eight years, I still have those dreams, only not as frequently. Sometimes I wake up with a peace in my heart because the dream revolved around some of the great times our family had. Other nights I awaken sweating and fearful of those old, negative feelings from the past that have crept into my head while I was sleeping. I have learned to accept them as a part of who I am and what I have been through.

Most of the time now, I can look back on my life and realize that God's grace was surrounding me at all times. This is true when I think about the joys of motherhood I was so lucky to witness, the beauty of the farm/ranch life we experienced, and the thrill of seeing each child leave the nest and spread his or her wings.

I met someone, by chance, who was so accepting of his life as it was at the moment and was living it with exuberance, not at all fearful of the aging process. This person changed my life in so many ways, but my sister was the one who turned it around for me.. Her death at thirty-nine years old made me realize that not one of us has a guarantee as to how long we will be here on earth. I become frustrated when I am around people who dread each year that brings them closer to the end. When my birthdays roll around, I am forever grateful to God that He lets me live. Hearing about birthday parties that use a black gloom-and-doom theme, like at fifty or sixty years when most of us are considered "over the hill," goes against this idea that life has an inevitable ending here on earth.

As soon as we are born, we all begin to die. We all know it to be true, but many of us actually live each day with dread and convince ourselves that we will live forever on this earth. Of course, there is a distinct difference between living your life with exuberance and waking each day looking forward to the good things life has to offer. But the joy and peace can be taken out of life if we are fearful of the aging process and stop at nothing to change our outward appearance so others will not know how old we are.

Many plastic surgeries have been performed unnecessarily just to cover up what God intended our bodies to do in old age. To me, "growing old gracefully" means staying as healthy as we can by watching our diets and exercising regularly, being socially active in a community or church, staying involved in children's lives, and being aware of the world outside our own front door.

Are you looking for God's grace in other people? Are you stopping long enough to be able to recognize grace when it is right before you? How often do we search this world for fulfillment on our own and believe that only we have the ability to make ourselves content?

Many churchgoers look to God to help them get through the demands of everyday life. Relationship issues, financial woes, workplace stressors, and child-rearing fears are all lessened when we seek His grace. Generation after generation of people send their children to Sunday worship when they are young with the hope of instilling a source of comfort and understanding of the world in which they are growing up.

Although a substantial amount of churches attended by millennials today seem to be nontraditional with praise bands belting out contemporary music, big-screen TVs, and even coffee shops right in the sanctuaries, they are still bringing their families along with them, and that is one way faith is integrated into the Generation Y households. This generation grew up with technology and social media at their fingertips. They are the most marketed-to individuals in the history of the United States.

Entertainment seems to be a high priority in a few of the churches I have attended. I witnessed a sense of need to be marketed to and having to be sold on the idea of religion among that group of people. Did God intend to provide our entertainment needs when we worship Him? Does His grace do the job of bringing these young adults and this "me" generation into the arms of the church and all it offers us? Would we keep the foundation of the church by doing this?

Many churches have conformed to what the millennial generation has demanded them to do—big video screens, less Bible reading, boisterous praise bands, and a movielike atmosphere. If it gets out a message to lost souls and puts their rear ends in the seats on Sunday, I think God would at least semi-approve.

> *Do not let Sunday be taken from you. If your soul*
> *has no Sunday, it becomes an orphan.*
> —Albert Schweitzer

Notes

Notes

_____

_____

_____

_____

_____

_____

_____

_____

_____

_____

_____

_____

_____

Chapter 2

Finding Grace in Our Friendships

February

A faithful friend is the medicine of life. And they that fear the Lord shall find him.

— Ecclesiastes 6:16

When we remember the friendships we formed over the years, we realize the diversity they all possessed. Starting from childhood, when the biggest influence who we were friends with were our parents or perhaps just geography, it lets us look back to them with wonder. Would these be people we would have chosen as our friends over any others? Did we learn from them? I had friendships from church, school, 4-H, and distant neighbors, as I lived in a rural community.

Actually my cousins were the first friendships I developed. We seemed to have a great deal in common and accepted each other as we were. All of this helped me walk down a long, restless, and wearisome path of trying to figure out who to choose among these friends and find the ones who would not only begin to show me the grace I would need when others were unkind or indifferent to me but would be steadfast in their friendship and hang on when it would become much easier to drift away.

Of course, the path became more complicated when I entered those emotional teen years. I was faced early on with a situation with a friend of mine who not only tested my faithfulness as a friend to her but kept it up and still does today. Staying near her and being by her side through the rough parts gave me a true sense of pleasure and pride. Worrying about what others were saying crept into my head many days through that journey with her. It would have been way easier to have dismissed her as one of those people to stay away from, but through God's grace, I did not falter. This whole episode taught me a great deal about who my friends really were and what that all meant in the challenging days of high school.

When I got married at eighteen and my college friends would come back to visit, our friendships changed. Or maybe I became different. Being married and raising a family was not even remotely on the minds of my fun-loving friends. That floundering feeling of being on the outside looking in was difficult for me. My friends who were living the college life, much different than my own life, made our conversations awkward with large gaps of silence in between. All of us had changed from our high school days. I am so fortunate that our friendships have sustained themselves through this period, but many do not.

My adult circle of friends changed as I became a mother of preschoolers. I find it funny how you can live right among people and meet them on the street but never really know them until all of you start parenting. I made friends through sports, school, and activities of our children, and many were young married couples with the same trials and tribulations I had. We formed a kinship because our lifestyles were similar.

After my marriage ended and I moved away from a greater share of my dearest friends, I developed new forms of graceful friendships. I only see some of these people at work. Others I met at a church retreat, and over a short weekend, we shared intimate details of our lives, causing us to share a graceful kinship for life. I also have many acquaintances that I only see once a week through a women's golf league. My adult friends from my past still keep in contact with me, and I am so grateful for that. Of course, today's technology makes it even easier to accomplish this.

God gives us the grace of friendship and expects us to nurture these relationships and to refuse to let them die. This takes a little hard work and unselfishness combined with some of God's grace. We, as humans, are not meant to be isolated from others and go through trials all alone. Of course, God tells us that He is all we need and we should go to Him with all that is troubling us. I also know that the Bible tells us to be friendly, caring, and full of grace toward others. Friendships are not just meant to give us support when we need it, but also to give us joy and love and fill our lives with gratification and merriment.

Pen Pals

Remember the soft, subtle, faint scents of lavender or violets, all sealed in a neatly wrapped package and tied with a big yellow or pink bow? It was my birthday gift at twelve years old! I found exquisitely boxed stationary filled with perfect papers and envelopes of the same design. It was a must-have if you were to have a pen pal in a distant city.

I chose my pen pal carefully from the list I read on the back of the *Pack-of-Fun* magazine that came to my door each month.

"She will be so impressed with my letter now," I said. "She will surely respond."

On those long summer days, I sat waiting for the rural mailman to drive his twenty-five- to forty-mile route into the countryside to deliver a letter back to me.

Of course, my penmanship meant a great deal to the correspondent and influenced her decision to respond. I didn't have any fancy markers, scented gel pens, or keyboard to type with. All I had was just my beautiful cursive writing with a pencil or pen lying around the house.

The first scribers used a quill dipped in ink. Large volumes of information in primitive libraries were painstakingly copied by hand, written in great detail. Then came the inventor of inks, and for a mere seven hundred years or so, the quill was the writing tool most often used. Goose feathers were very common, but swan feathers were of premium grade. These would only last about a week and needed to be replaced.

Around 1950, the ink pen was introduced. Parker Brothers introduced the first ballpoint pen that was supposed to last at least two years. The Bic Company was also a major manufacturer of the pen. Pencils have their own history as well. Many children learned to write with the number two pencil. The mechanical pencil is still used today. Writers are given unlimited choices to jot down their thoughts and mail them off to their dear ones.

Unfortunately those days are only a memory. At every yard or estate sale I witness, at least one box of stationary on the table, waiting for some buyer to pick it up and send off a letter to a friend. I think I will set out the box of colored envelopes and paper on my desk (as I couldn't resist), just to relive a brief history of my pen pal days. Doesn't it brighten our day when we receive a handwritten note or letter sent to us in a person's own handwriting on a beautiful piece of notepaper?

Signing Our Name

Letter writing in this century is a lost art form. As someone who loves to receive cards and notes from friends and loved ones, I am doing a poor job of returning the favor. Nowadays I have to physically force myself to write a letter to my son who is overseas. I know how very much my letters bring him joy, and he looks forward to cards and care packages. The Internet has changed my mind about using snail mail, and I now rely on technology to be able to connect with most of my current friends. I have hung on to a few of my letters I've received in the past. They are fun to go back through and read from my embarrassing teenage years.

My best friend in high school and I lived only about thirty miles apart, but in the summer, it meant a long-distance phone charge to call each other. I was never allowed to make those calls, so we wrote letters to each other every week. When my oldest son went to boot camp, I watched the mailbox every day, hoping to hear from him. When the phone or the Internet is taken from us, letter writing holds importance to us.

Current news articles talk about letting the cursive writing curriculum leave the school system. This has been met with some controversy. But the art of writing the English alphabet is not just for the purpose of signing our name on a dotted line. It can be beneficial to write a heartfelt letter to someone you care deeply for or just some casual friend you would like to cheer up. We can't, for instance, send a birthday or sympathy card without signing our name at the bottom. I'm quite sure many elderly citizens would love to receive a handwritten letter from one of their relatives. That would be the grace that God has given to us so we can shower each other with blessings and improve each other's lives.

> *Letter writing is the only device*
> *For combining solitude with good company.*
> —Lord Byron

Notes

Notes

Chapter 3

Spacious Grace

March

Do not lay up for yourselves treasures on earth, where moth and rust destroy and where thieves break in and steal, but layup, for yourselves, treasures in heaven, where neither moth nor rust destroys and where thieves do not break in and steal. For where your treasure is, there your heart will be also.

—Matthew 6:19–21

Is your life as abundantly full of grace as you hoped it would be? What objects take up the greatest amount of space in your life? The more I have been scanning neighborhoods in search of a good bargain, the more I have witnessed our tremendous American abundance. I am thoroughly amazed at the amount of toys, clothing, books, and endless excess that are either thrown out or sold at a yard sale. Even if we are doing very well financially, does it really do our families any good to overindulge in accessible pleasures? Of course, it never leaves me feeling this way when I see a big tote full of books that people are willing to sell. At least it lets me know that their households are attempting to educate their inhabitants.

Moderation is a key to living a life full of grace. Of course, some pleasures are not meant to skip, and we can certainly afford to give our lives joy and peace. God doesn't intend for our lives to lack the simple things that we have at our convenience. Chocolate is good for us, but too much can be unhealthy. Children are naturally immoderate. They want to watch the same movie over and over. They want to eat too much of one thing, and they lack restraint in expressing emotion. Part of maturity is learning to say no to oneself.

Children in homes where money is no deterrent to what they think they need do not always grow up with the necessary monetary restraints put on them. Their adult life can be a difficult road if their future spouse has grown up knowing how to put limits on spending. Ever-growing conflicts about money are a major concern in a growing number of households. The Bible also tells us to share our wealth and abundance with others who are less fortunate.

Make Room for My Stuff

"Space to work, space to breathe, and space for all my stuff!" Isn't that the exact words that we tell ourselves will make our whole lives whole or complete?

When I was younger, I occupied as little space as possible. I shared one bedroom with four of my other siblings and slept curled up in a full-sized bunk bed every night with them as well.

We had one dresser, as I recall, and we had very little clothing. It sure made picking out the right outfit for the day fairly simple and easy.

But of course, all of that has changed. We are better off than our parents' generation. We have the means to give our own children much more than we had. Are they better people for it? We try to tell ourselves that.

My family also yearned for more space. When I was almost eight, we poured a basement, and the four of us girls acquired two more bedrooms to accommodate our growing stuff. For a while, it worked. The biggest problem facing us in the matter of space was which sister I had to share my room with.

Most of my friends went to college and occupied a small space in a dorm room, and I got married and managed to live in a three-room house in the country. Then as our children arrived, we excitedly moved into a larger space. We thought we were in a mansion, compared to what we were used to.

This three-bedroom house, however, didn't have a basement and had limited storage for all of our stuff. Three children later, we found ourselves with an infant in the living room with all of his possessions in or under his crib or, most often, on the floor all over the house. Many days we yearned for more space. But days went on, and our children grew. And every time we moved after that, we looked for a house with more room because we had acquired so much: more clothing, more tools, more books, and more *stuff*.

If you look around a neighborhood and witness the older homes in a small town that were built around the 1950s, you will notice almost all of them only have a single-car garage attached. A great number of these families also had very well-built homes.

They were built to last with little regard to how they looked or how well they functioned. Back then, that is all people felt they needed. We bought one of these houses in 2000, and the first thing we did was add a beautiful, new two-car garage. Finally we had more space.

Is this the stuff life should be made of? All of this spatial thinking affects people's lifelong decisions—whether we purchase or build new homes, how we entertain our guests, or if we accumulate more and more. This is how we become measured by our neighbors, peers, or family. What we forget sometimes is how very often toward the end of our lives, we are forced to move to smaller spaces and downsize and keep the things that mean the most to us.

In all of this transition, I have witnessed my grandmother and other relatives (the older generation) who still lead very happy and fulfilling lives by becoming simple people, even occupying the same space in this world they were born with and becoming closer to God and their own true values.

I complained that I had no shoes until I met a man with no feet.
—Persian proverb

Notes

Notes

_____

_____

_____

_____

_____

_____

_____

_____

_____

_____

_____

_____

_____

_____

_____

Grace is when God gives us what we don't deserve and
Mercy is when he doesn't give us what we do deserve.

Chapter 4

The Lord Gives Us a Grace Period

April

To everything there is a season, and a time to every purpose under the heavens. A time to be born and a time to die; A time to plant and a time to pluck up that which is planted

—Ecclesiastes 3:1–2

Webster's dictionary defines a grace period as a period of time beyond a due date during which a financial obligation may be met without penalty or cancellation. Does God grant us a grace period to carry out the words of scripture? Does He extend our time on earth so we receive many second chances to redeem ourselves? Do we get extra time to work out our differences with each other? Many times we feel as if we have all of the time in the world and our lives are boring with days on end of drudgery, doing the same job or the same menial tasks around the house? At other times, hours or days seem to fly by, giving us an excuse for not showing the extra love and concern that we know others can use.

Whichever the case, God gives all of us the same number of hours in a day to use as we see fit. I know other people have given me several grace periods. They have been very patient with me. This is all due to their forgiveness of my sins in much the same way that God forgives. The month of April in this book is about the importance of time and how we use it. All of us get the same twenty-four hours a day to spend our time on this earth. I once heard these are three of the hardest things to do while we inhabit our space on earth:

1. to repay hatred with kindness
2. to admit we are wrong
3. to include the excluded

Why is it so difficult to repay our enemies? It is much less difficult to ignore others or go out of our way to avoid the people who have rubbed us the wrong way. Why is it so difficult to admit our mistakes? God says we should come to Him with our sins and repent. It is much easier to talk to God about our faults than to own up to them with the people we love or who supposedly love us back. Why is it so hard to include others who are oftentimes excluded? It is easier to ignore them or leave it up to someone else to take charge rather than risk being ridiculed because of whom we associate with.

Notice every answer we give ourselves has the word "easier" in it. Through the grace of God, we can begin to work on the harder things in life rather than take the simpler path. Our time on this earth is limited. We all know that we start to die as soon as we are born. No one talks about death as much as life, but dying is right there in front of us, whether it's today or years from now. So how we spend our time on earth will reflect how we spend eternity.

> *When you get into a tight place and everything goes*
> *against you, till it seems as though you could not*
> *hang on a minute longer, never give up then, for that*
> *is just the place and time that the tide will turn.*
>
> —Harriet Beecher Stowe

Making Time

Time can stand still, it can march on, or we can travel back in it. But how are we telling time? If you lived long ago when a timepiece was a status symbol, think of one of your first gifts that you might have longed for. It was meant to be cared for, admired, and wished for. It was usually carried in a breast or pants pocket or in a waistcoat. These true treasures now lay in a box, still workable but not used nearly as much. The pocket watch was often revered by young boys of all walks of life, given to them by a special grandfather and passed down from generation to generation to be cherished and used as a gentle reminder of the time spent with their loved ones. I have come across these relics from the past at numerous yard sales where I live at this time.

The basic wristwatch soon took the place of a pocket style and was a necessity in the years I was growing up. If you didn't wear one when you were younger, you fully expected one to be wrapped up under your tree or as a birthday gift by the time you became fourteen. It didn't need to be fancy as long as the two hands could tell you the time of day. After all, your parents expected you to know when to come in for dinner or be back from the swimming pool or your friend's house. No longer were you living your daily life without the knowledge of time.

Then the new age of digital timekeeping brought us to a quick glance at the wrist, and amazingly "6:15" was right there in front of you. No more relying on the time-telling methods you learned in second grade. What a time-saving concept! The world of wristwatches then became even more glamorous. They could match your wardrobe, be laden with jewels, have a stretchy band, display petite or oversized numbers, or be waterproof. Many of us wouldn't have thought to leave the house without our wristwatch on.

Guess what method we are using to keep track of time now? I haven't worn a wristwatch for at least the last ten years. I don't even own one now. No longer do I need to browse the jewelry aisles for a brand-new, stylish, exquisite watch. We do know that the wristwatch manufacturers are definitely witnessing a big decline in their production. If I forget my cell phone when I leave home in the morning, I now have left my timepiece at home as well. This has happened to me on more than one occasion. But I can always check the time on my radio dial in my car or my computer screen at the office, so it's not a total loss. Do I even look at a clock on the wall at work? Yes, but not as much as I used to.

Time is not meant to be watched minute by minute. Take a look back at my high school biology classroom. On the wall above the blackboard, right underneath the big, black clock in enormous, bold letters, it stated "Time Will Pass. Will You?" I have said those exact words numerous times since.

I realize that, when I retire from my company after twenty-five years, they won't be giving me that gold watch that was so envied way back when. They might not even acknowledge the fact you worked for them that long. Instead I wish they could come up with a way to give us more free time. Perhaps, they could wrap it all up neatly with a big certificate of achievement that gives us permission to relax and enjoy the good stuff allowing time to be on our side. But would we use it wisely?

What Special Day Is It Today?

In America, we can wake up early every single day, look at a calendar, and declare it's a special day! Here are a few popular days you might not have heard of yet:

- January 19: National Popcorn Day
- January 25: Opposites Day
- February 7: Charles Dickens's Day
- February 22: Be Humble Day
- March 22: Goof-Off Day
- March 26: Make Up Your Own Holiday Day
- April 19–25: National Secretary's Week
- October 16 Boss's Day

Now I am not against celebrating any of our federally observed, established-by-the-government, national holidays. But we are now literally inundated with holidays or special events that are meant to introduce us to new causes or promote a certain event. It seems a bit overwhelming to all who try to keep up with the overload of these well-meaning dates that we are expected to add to our already overscheduled calendars.

Lisa Marie

Take Veteran's Day, Native American Day, Columbus Day, and Martin Luther King Day, for example. I still would like to see more schoolchildren in class those days and be told the real reason they are celebrating it. President's Day falls on a Monday every year now, so certain workers can get a three-day weekend. All of those Monday holidays have lost their effectiveness.

Mother's Day and Father's Day have been around a long time, but they can often just add to a person's grief and suffering from a loss that is hard to bear. When the advertisements from the media insist on these happiness holidays, many people feel end up feeling worse. Young mothers and fathers who have lost an infant might experience greater pain when those famous days come around.

Christmas Day has become a stressful time, and blended families try to make that exact day perfect when, in reality, it is just another day. The get-together should be observed when it works best for everyone. Finding that perfect time, however, can also be a burden on our loved ones. In fact, when Christmas starts in August for retailers, the excitement has worn off for many of us by December. Did you know that biblical evidence points to the actual birth of Jesus as being in late autumn in September or October? My point is that it is just another date on the calendar. God wants us to celebrate Jesus's birth, but anytime will do just fine.

Maybe our focus should be on the celebrations, not the dates. And if Valentine's Day is for lovers and you happen to be single, all the hype does nothing but make you sad. Christians all over the world recognize National Day of Prayer. Does it entice people to pray in abundance on just that one day? Or does it light a spark under some not so prayerful believers so their prayer life becomes a habit and they increase their relationship with the Lord? Our relationship with God should include an everyday prayer life as that is what he is seeking from all of us.

When the retail stores begin selling cards, trinkets, or decorations the day after a holiday is over for up to 80 percent off, it tells me the value of all this is diminished. We look to the next holiday coming up and start planning that one the very next week.

Originally I thought by not observing all of these special holidays on the exact day that everyone else celebrated them should be considered a wrong way to live. But over time, after I met someone who doesn't live by the dates on the calendar to celebrate, I have begun to receive random gifts, flowers, and cards at unexpected times of the year, and not knowing when they will come is a big surprise. It made me realize that this is the only way to live.

Holy Sunday

We have all come to accept the seventh day of the week as a time for work, travel, competitions, and other unholy things. I do not remember my parents' generation ever working very hard on a Sunday. Yes, they were farmers, and the usual chores never ended, but my grandpa rarely missed Sunday church services or ever a church activity in the afternoon. A special day was reserved for a drive to the river, a visit from relatives, or just a day of relaxation. They observed God's holy day as He requested it.

By some miracle, my grandparents managed to get their shopping, housework, fieldwork, and other deeds of great importance done during the workweek. Actually that's somewhat of a miracle considering they didn't have all the convenient appliances and farming equipment that we use today.

Think of all of the time-saving methods we take for granted now. My mother's wash was done in a wringer washer, the dishes were done by hand (frequently by my sisters and me), farm chores took many hours of physical labor, and tractors were not as huge as they are now. Haying or silage cutting might take a real precedent over Sunday services too. Lambing and calving season meant that someone needed to miss church once or twice as well.

About the time my children were in middle school, I noticed a slight shift in a different direction when youth wrestling tournaments were scheduled on Sundays. This caused a conflict with parents who had to make a choice about what their priorities were. My children at that time also might have taken in a Sunday evening 4-H meeting.

Now the newspapers are filled with sports, nonreligious activities, and any number of excuses to never take a rest and just enjoy the seventh day of the week. Some businesses are closed on Sunday now, but these are very few. It is a rarity. In fact, the TV news lists boredom busters every Sunday morning so just in case, God forbid, we would run out of things to do.

Is it any wonder we are more stressed and our children have very little time to just be children? If we are forced to have to choose between Sunday school and a sporting event, maybe we have lost our sense of what our families really lack, time together to hang out without any scheduled activities.

Before this time in our lives, you couldn't even get gas or groceries on a Sunday in our small town. Would I want to give up that luxury? Not a chance. But having that capability forces others to work on Sunday as well. Even I have been frustrated when I couldn't go to a craft store when the rest of my family was watching football as I thought it sounded way better than four hours of TV sports.

But we complacently go about our fast-paced lives, never taking solitude that God offers us. I even see people in church on their cellphones, never really listening to the message. Our present generation will not protest this at all because they do not know any other way. The short breathers we take now will not make up for the daylong rest that God intended for us every week.

The time for showing God's grace to others is the day you do it without intention, reminders from Hallmark, or any reason other than the fact you love that person and want him or her to know it. The extra-special times I have been sent a just-thinking-of-you card or flowers for no apparent reason seem to stick out in my mind. Mass marketing of cards, flowers, gifts, and more on these so-called special days leaves many people feeling like their loved ones have forgotten them when the day comes and they haven't been recognized. I would like to think my loved ones know my feelings through my interactions with them on the nontraditional days as well.

Nine-tenths of wisdom consists of being wise in time.
—Theodore Roosevelt (1858–1882)

Notes

Notes

Chapter 5

Social Grace

May

For where two or three are gathered together in my name, there am I in the midst of them.

Matthew 18:20

If we want to live in harmony with others, we need to show some form of acceptable social grace. In finishing or charm schools during the midcentury, classes were generally taught on etiquette, proper manners, and grace. When we exhibit behavior above the normal manners and grace that the general public puts forth, we often make that difference in our employment advancement or even in an election process. Exemplary social graces would more likely win out at employment offices, company social functions, or any adult gatherings. People who realize the importance of manners are usually regarded with a higher respect, and God wants us to mimic that grace that He gives us.

How many of us have been impatient in traffic and lashed out our anger at the other driver? Do we hold open the door for others when we enter a public place? Most of the time, I find people to be in a big hurry, thus putting forth little effort in their regard for others. Saying "please" and "thank you" goes a long way and, more often than not, can become a lifelong habit.

The social grace that God intends for us to use is much more than simple manners. It is the lifestyle we strive to lead in our relation with our fellow man. This relationship takes place on a daily basis as we come in contact with family, coworkers, neighbors, church congregations, and people we meet on the street or our personal journey that we all take.

At times, we have to change our whole persona and put forth an effort to respect our waitress at the restaurant or a janitor in our building, those workers who go unnoticed as we go about our daily lives. Younger people are witnessing how we react in these situations when we overreact, are impatient, and generally remain unconcerned for others. We also need to realize there are many lonely people in this world who would like nothing more than to be treated to a short visit from someone to help cure their anguish. There are children who are hurting as well and could use a strong dose of our grace as the Lord works through us. To show up and be there for them doesn't take much time, but it does take a commitment and some excellent people skills as well. Taking the focus off ourselves and giving to others is part of that social grace that God is referring to.

Social Clubs

My mother hosted a club party at our house every few months back when I was growing up. The dessert had to be just right, and the small finger sandwiches were made so carefully. Usually it was a chicken salad or a ground roast beef sandwich served elegantly on a vintage glass snack tray. Mints and peanuts were also not overlooked. Every modern woman of the 1950s acquired a set of trays for just such an occasion. The afternoon club get-togethers served a purpose not well-known in our modern times. My daughters of the millenial generation now find coffee shops and restaurants to meet their friends and to stay connected. But this social club form of get-togethers was so much more meaningful because it helped connect the women living in rural areas in a time when cell phones, text messages, computers, or Facebook was not an option.

I can still remember racing home from country school in the afternoon to either my mom's or my grandma's house and seeing the yard filled with cars and ladies sitting around the living room enjoying each other's company. I loved those days, as the after-school snack was always extra-special and we were welcomed to sample the leftovers. If some other neighbor lady was hosting the club that day, we got to go to their house after school, and that was always a treat.

Women who belonged to the social club made sure their house was in good, clean shape, and it became an important part of the lives on the prairies of South Dakota. Many recipes were traded, child-rearing advice was given out, and sometimes quilts were worked on, but overall the feeling of community it generated among women who lived miles away from each other benefitted from the socializing it provided. Even though most families communicated through a party line on their telephone and could often hear the news of the week via eavesdropping to others' conversations, the social club brought women face-to-face with their neighbors in a friendly, happy environment. I suspect it also provided sympathy and compassion when one of the women was experiencing pain in her life.

When I got married and moved to a wonderful community, the first thing I got was an invitation to attend a club meeting. They put on a baby shower for me when I had my first child as well. Most of the time, there was no real agenda other than to see each other and socialize. I know we all could use a small dose of that in our busy lives.

Socializing

How much do you go out to eat in a week? How about in a month? When you do go out, are you conscious of the amount of time you spend in the restaurant/bar and how much work the people of the service industry really do?

I read an article last week about the amount of time it was taking for people to come in the door of their favorite restaurant and then to leave again. The article quoted a survey taken ten years ago and compared it to the present time. In 2005, the average time spent was forty minutes. Today in 2015, the average time was one hour and forty minutes. Why so long? Is it because the restaurant is busier and can't handle the extra work involved?

Think about this. See if any part of this scenario has any

resemblance to the way you, as an adult, act when you go to a restaurant. The waiter or waitress comes over to your table of six. Every one of you would most likely be on your cell phones. The waiter or waitress politely asks if he or she can get you anything to drink. When he or she comes back with your drinks and lays the menus on your table, half of you put your cell phones on top of the menu and continue to scroll. After about ten minutes the waiter/waitress comes again to ask if you are ready to place your order. Of course, no one has taken the time to look, so the waiter or waitress has to come back a second time. Finally your food order is brought to the table. Of course, half of you feel the need to take a picture of the food first and show it to your social media friends.

When all of you are finally finished eating, the waiter or waitress comes back and asks your table if he or she can get you anything else. The night would not be complete without someone at the table wanting the waiter or waitress to take a quick photo of the group to again send to social media. Of course, most of the time, he or she has to take another photo because that was not suitable and couldn't possibly be sent out to all of your friends.

Do you see how this evening out, just to enjoy each other's company, has become still another reason to involve our phones? I want to declare a National No-Phone Day where we all go out to a nice, classy restaurant and actually talk face-to-face with our friends and family without any of the (unnecessary) distractions that we have placed on ourselves and others around us. By the way, tip your service personnel, please, when you do go out to eat. Everything he or she has to contend with is not in his or her original job description.

Graciousness abides in a person's soul when he or she manages to forgive others easily, spreads kindness, is merciful to others, and welcomes others with courtesy. Gracious can also mean to have tact or good taste and be elegant. Warm welcomes to one another shows a person has graciousness.

As important as using these social graces are to our environments, it seems that our hurried, fast-paced life is not allowing us to be fully aware of the significance. If we learn these manners when we are younger, it seems to come more easily, and we do the right thing without even thinking about it. In my pursuit of grace, I found I must have witnessed many gracious adults and the way they interacted with others, as I recognize it when I see it.

> *Always do right. That will gratify some*
> *people and astonish the rest.*
> —Mark Twain (1835–1910)

Notes

_____

_____

_____

_____

_____

_____

_____

_____

_____

_____

_____

_____

_____

Notes

Chapter 6

Heavenly State of Grace

June

By whom also we have access by faith into this grace wherein we stand, and rejoice in hope of the glory of God.

—Romans 5:2

What state of grace are you in today? Does happiness become who you are, and does it stay with you even in your darker days? Most people have to get to this stage in their life where they are in a proper state of health, a respectable financial state, and a stable state of affairs. This usually comes with understanding what does and doesn't work in our lives, which takes a greater share of our life to discover. When we understand this, we do things differently because we can better predict what the outcomes will be and how our actions will affect our consequences in life.

Unsettled

Today's Americans in the age group of twenty-five to forty years are currently trying to raise a family, land a job (or keep a good one), prepare for retirement, and keep up with the necessary insurance premiums, all while attempting to watch over their children and trying to protect them from the negative effects of the Internet or the corruptive news media that's filling their thoughts. Maybe this group can best be described as feeling somewhat unsettled.

This term also refers to the youth in 2016 and their feelings, some of whom go to school each day in fear. Maybe not on the surface, but inside of their young minds, the voices are telling them that they are not completely safe in their classrooms either. Now they are asked to participate in regular lockdown procedures alongside the normal fire or tornado drills, innocently unaware of the very dangers that may occur between the hours of eight and three. These unsettled feelings can be thought of as the opposite of settled.

Think about this when you remember the challenges of our pioneers, who ventured across this great nation searching for nothing more than to become settlers. It wasn't just the land they sought, but stability, roots, and a home for their families. Have we sacrificed even half as much as they did? Americans are enjoying all of the best appliances, available and unlimited food supplies, unmatched health care (even though unaffordable), and instant communication at our fingertips. But are we feeling settled now that we have come so far?

Today's children are some of the more resilient youth than any other generation before them. This can be a great attribute.

It can often make our youth stronger and more ready to meet the challenges facing them today. But other times, when they are witnessing their parents in that unsettled state, it can trickle down to them as well and have lasting negative effects on their psyche. It is happening in a rather subtle way as they are uprooted and moved away from their support system of family and friends.

When I left my hometown after forty-five years and moved five hours west, I spent the first year in transition and faced the unsettled feelings of my ancestors. What I was looking to find was stability, roots, friendships, a faith community, and a sense of freedom. Much of the satisfaction I began to feel came from somewhere inside of myself. Education, faith, and new friendships also added to that settled feeling. My frustrations seem minor compared to my grandparents' deep struggles.

Millennials have the world at their fingertips. They prefer urban centers where they have access to shopping, restaurants, and offices. It can be said that sixty percent of this age group in 2014 did not strive to live in the suburbs with a white picket fence and a house with a mortgage.[2]

So here we are as Americans in 2016. Are we looking for our government to settle us? Do we expect our law enforcement to settle us and keep us safe from harm? Perhaps it's our boss or our job that will settle us and bring us security? Are we even close to succeeding?

Perhaps if we choose to look more inside of ourselves and begin to care more about our neighbors' and family's well-beings and then start to care less about our own overpriced and larger homes or vehicles that we can somehow only manage to make

---

[2] Refer to www.nielsen.com.

the monthly payments on or our newest smart technology that seems to detach us even further from our personal relationships, then and only then will this unsettled generation feel increasingly secure or, more importantly, content.

Is this the state of grace we want our youth to be in?

> *This is a state of grace.*
> *This is a worthwhile fight.*
> *Love is a ruthless game*
> *Unless you play it good and right.*
> —Taylor Swift, "State of Grace"

Notes

Notes

Seek God's will in all you do, and He
will show you the path to take.

Chapter 7

Falling From Grace/Disgrace

July

But he giveth more grace. Wherefore he said, God resisted the proud, but giveth grace unto the humble.

—James 4:6

More and more times in my life, I feel God's presence all around me. I hear this when people are in need of change or feeling anxious about something negative in their lives. God's sense of humor, at times, can delight me as well. Falling from grace has occurred in everyone's life at certain moments. How we move forward and when we realize that we are only human and God's forgiveness puts us in His grace will determine how we handle the next situation that arises. When otherwise good and righteous people lose their sense of right and wrong, the outer face they portray to others can be nothing like what they are feeling on the inside.

Friends might respond to the news by saying, "That doesn't

sound anything like the man I know and love. Why would he do that?"

What temptations do we give into, and how strong are we when enticements stare us directly in the face? God lets us fall so we can pick ourselves back up and hopefully learn from the experiences. He wants us to ask Him for forgiveness, and He made sure His dying on the cross totally exonerated our sins. This is His grace that He has promised to us.

A Small Fall from Grace

My earliest memory of a fall from grace happened when I was in about sixth grade. I went to a one-room schoolhouse with only about fifteen other students total. My teacher took her job very seriously, and looking back, I have realized how much I truly did learn from her. Of course, going to school for eight hours a day in the same room as your siblings meant that whatever happened with you, good or bad, would sure enough follow you home too. That left me somewhat cautious about my behavior.

About this time in my life, my awkward shyness around adults began to change. It seemed I was feeling bolder and smarter every day. Is it around middle school that we begin to resist authority to some degree? My partners in crime that I hung out with at this small school were becoming increasingly belligerent to our teacher. It never did feel suitable for me on the inside, but I was also struggling to fit in and trying to overcome that good-girl image as well.

The day I left a small, rolled-up note that I had wrote to my friend and the teacher intercepted it first was that first fall from grace day for me. The note was short, not so sweet, and right to the point, and it included a swear word about the teacher that was much easier to write than to commit to out loud. I have carried this little secret around for a long time. Every time I would see her after that, even years later, that fateful day she thought I hated her would come to my mind.

In truth, I did not hate her. I respected her more and more after that. The look on her face when she read the note was enough to make me realize how much I had hurt her.

It Was Bound to Happen

It was a typical summer day when I decided to go golfing alone, something I never dreamed would ever give me as much pleasure as it does now. The full sunshine of this beautiful blue sky morning took over my whole body. I was feeling downright proud of my score on the first four holes. The last few years of golf lessons were finally paying off. Up ahead of me, however, on the sixth hole was an elderly woman golfing all alone with a cart, but moving along as slow as a tortoise. I, however, always walked this course. Not wimpy. No, not me. The whole experience was adding to my goal of getting back in shape after the long Midwestern winter I had just endured. This seasoned golfer ahead of me was taking her dear, sweet time at each hole and didn't seem at all concerned I was directly behind her, forcing me to stop and wait at each green.

"Patience, God. Please give me patience," I spoke silently.

As all golfers know, the waiting game can throw off a good golfer's approach faster than greased lightning. Waiting and waiting. Naturally, excuses like those come a dime a dozen when we are at the golf course.

So on I went and finally got to the ninth hole, which is over Rapid Creek on an easy par three. Anxious to complete my final hole with a thirty-five score and call my friend to brag about it again, I watched this sweet, elderly golfer tee it up. Her first and second ball went right in the creek. This hole had taken her already about fifteen minutes from start to finish. My eye rolling was kept to myself, an act of which I am not proud to mention.

Now we proceed to the important part of this story. I had not whacked a ball in this creek all summer and maybe only one time last summer. That was how much my skills had improved. I was so overconfident it might kill me. My patience was gone by now, and I was not too proud of the words going through my head.

She finally got her ball to go across the creek, and I stepped up to the reds. Over the creek, my ball flew and landed right on the edge of the green. I didn't even wait for her to slowly get over the bridge and finish her golf day.

I finished with a thirty-eight and felt like it was well worth my time even though I was not impressed with the delays I had to endure. End of story? Not quite.

The bigger the ego, the harder it falls. Our God and His brilliant sense of humor I mentioned earlier showed up the next day at executive women's league play. Still feeling like I had this golf thing all figured out, I made par on four holes and had a really nice thirty-three going into the ninth hole. Oh yeah. The creek, remember? No problem. My first ball hit the leaves of the overhanging tree and splashed playfully straight into the creek. It was a fluke. It just couldn't be true. My second ball took a big splash as well, and it lay at the bottom of Rapid Creek with a defeated look on its dimpled face. Now I was hitting for a five stroke and ending up with an eight on the ninth hole.

"All right, God," I said to myself. "I got this."

I'm a slow learner. I was starting to fall off my ladder of grace, but no one knew how far I'd fallen except me. I can't even describe the inconceivable way my egotistical, selfish mind started reeling from the day before. I took a step back and realized a few things about my life and how I looked at the aging process. Patience is always a virtue, and showing respect for my elders are at the top of the list of things I learned on this golf course. Why did it take so long for me to figure it all out? I guess we are all just a work in progress. We all fall from grace occasionally, but God helps us back up that ladder, one rung at a time.

A proud man is always looking down on things and people;
And, of course, as long as you are looking down,
You can't see something that is above you.
—C.S. Lewis

Notes

Notes

Chapter 8

My Saving Grace

August

But grow in grace, and in the knowledge of our Lord and Savior Jesus Christ. To him be glory both now and forever. Amen.

—2 Peter 3:18

It's easier to give grace when we realize we desperately need grace ourselves. But how many of us put others' needs above our own? With the state of the world being as it is, the time is more critical to put forth kindness and grace to each other. By acknowledging our differences, just like Christ did, we can begin to accept others and have a tolerance for people who live a different lifestyle from our own.

How much grace do you witness in your own neighborhood or your daily life as you go about your business of making a living? It is not just about our manners we use as we politely open a door for an elderly senior citizen or slow down and let someone pass us in traffic. If we are to duplicate God's grace and begin to change our communities, we will have to go out of our comfort zone and bring that unforeseen joy and spontaneous smile to someone's face when he or she least expects it.

When this kind of grace is granted toward others without a moment of hesitation, it is an amazing performance to witness, well worth an encore. Most people who do this, however, do not want to be noticed or mentioned or even revealed to anyone else. That is not the motive of their actions. They do not seek others' acceptance. The sheer joy on someone's face is all the grandeur they desire.

If we look around more at the world outside of our own front door, the opportunities to express subtle grace and graciousness to others is right there, waiting for us to shower our neighbors with all of our subtle gestures. People of all ages are capable of this precious gift.

Subtle Grace

I was privileged to witness grace shown to others several times over the last year. It was early December in the Midwest where the nights can be brutal if your home is outdoors and you are not prepared. I was out enjoying an evening with this carefree, endearing gentleman when, walking along, we both looked down at the ground at the same time and saw a ten-dollar bill on the sidewalk.

After an evening of a few drinks and laughter, I thought this was our bonus and never once considered who had lost it or how much it might have meant to him or her. Was it a single mother who watched every dime she spent? Well, of course, my friend picked it up.

We ended our evening shortly after, and on our way to my house, we drove by a park with more than a homeless persons laid out on the ground. When my friend parked the car but didn't return immediately, I wondered what he was up to. He finally walked in, and I asked him what the delay was.

And he stated matter-of-factly, "I gave a woman our sleeping bag that was in your trunk and the ten-dollar bill that wasn't really mine to begin with. So someone has paid it forward tonight without even realizing it."

This was God's grace playing out right in front of me. I slowly figured out that this same man must live his life a little bit different way than most of us, as I witnessed his grace and generosity many times over.

We were at a sports bar with my adult children watching the NFL playoffs in December. A much-loved Seattle team was playing, and this excited football fan wearing his famed jersey his sister had sent him from Seattle thought they were surely going to the Super Bowl. Life was good, they were winning, and we were having a great time with my children who loved the Vikings.

Not far from our table sat a teenage mentally handicapped girl in a wheelchair. She was an obvious Seattle fan and screamed and hollered with every great play they made. After the game was over, I looked for my friend and couldn't find him anywhere. When the crowd in the bar had settled down, I searched the room and found my friend talking to the parents of the teenage girl. She was sporting his prized jersey with the biggest smile on her face they had ever seen. The mom had tears streaming down her face, and her dad just looked bewildered.

One of the best moments of all was seeing her face. She knew exactly what he had done, and my adult children were stunned. Could we all be this generous and take the focus off our own needs, maybe just a little?

There was an article in the newspaper months later about this same man who had overheard some women talking about a quilt that was raffled off at a cancer walk the night before. The woman who stated she really wanted to win it didn't realize the gentleman I have been describing earlier actually did win it, and it happened to be out in his vehicle. He said he asked himself what he was going to do with this beautiful quilt but speculated no further.

This chance meeting of these two individuals was somewhat coincidental. But I believe God's grace had a hand in it all. He brought those two together at just the right moment and brightened this lady's day. She had recently been diagnosed with cancer and was hoping to win the quilt so she could pass it on to her daughter.

Once again, without hesitation, an act of grace appeared and took very little effort. But the consequences were astronomical. To live our lives like this, we first have to get out of our egotistical world and join the ranks of the members of this society who actually understand why we are placed here and why God tries to teach us His ways.

> *We often receive significant but subtle blessings,*
> *That are not always what we expect,*
> *And can easily be overlooked.*
> —Elder David A. Bednar

Notes

Notes

Chapter 9

Amazing Grace

September

O sing unto the Lord a new song: sing unto the Lord, all the earth. Sing unto the Lord, bless his name; shew forth his salvation from day to day.

—Psalm 96:1–2

Musical Grace

How much music fills the gap in your everyday thoughts? When does a certain tune take you back to a prior time period in your life? I honestly cannot think of a time when music was not a part of my life. This is somewhat hard to believe if you know me at all, as I never got a chance to learn to play an instrument and my limited piano skills are not what I would have preferred. I cannot carry a tune in a pail either, although that doesn't keep me from singing if I get a chance. Nevertheless, I do not go a day without music either on the radio, in my earbuds, or on my new turntable.

Albums and record players are making a comeback. I sure wish I would have held onto more of my records that I purchased for under a dollar when I was about eleven or twelve years old. Often I would buy a forty-five record with one song on the front and another on the back and play them over and over. One summer I purchased the cherished Monkees' seventy-eight RPM record "I'm a Believer," and I stuck it up in the back window of our vehicle while I went to the swimming pool. It must have been almost ninety degrees that day, but the pool seemed like heaven. I was on a natural high and couldn't wait to get home and play my little record. But when I got back home, I was astonished to see the hot summer sun had diminished my prized songs into a rippled, distorted disaster.

Specific songs can take me back to my youth in a blink of an eye. Bible school was attended every summer and usually lasted from nine to three for an entire week. Those teachers had a real challenge on their hands to keep us focused when we would have much rather been outdoors doing outdoor things, like riding our bikes or swimming. But the music we sang was so fun and has stayed with me my whole life. "Michael, Row the Boat Ashore" and "I Got the Joy, Joy, Joy" will always take me back there to that little church on the hill where my friends gathered to worship Jesus.

When I started elementary school, I was blessed to have a teacher who had musical talent as well as her teaching skills. In country schools, it was customary for instructors to teach the whole spectrum of education, including music, PE, and art. I will never hear an accordion without seeing my teacher standing up in front of us and playing tunes such as "This Land is Your Land" or "Red River Valley." She played the piano and knew every song from the red songbook that we loved to sing. The older boys pretended not to enjoy the songs or the accompaniment, but our teacher kept playing them with zest.

Young Citizens League (YCL) had a march song, and it fills me with pride, although I rarely hear it anymore. "We March and We Sing, Our Voices Ring, Young Citizens Are We" had a ring to it that has stuck with me and jogs my memory to that one-room country school that we walked to where I learned good citizenship, patriotism, and a true, respectful love for my country.

Music filled my life more and more as a young teen. My aunt, who was only two years older than I was, held dance parties, and we played Name That Tune many afternoons at her house. All you needed to do was lift the needle off the record at intervals and then try to guess the name of the song. *American Bandstand* was rarely missed at my house, even though it required someone scaling the roof to turn the antennae so we could pull in ABC channel 5. When the Beatles came on *Ed Sullivan*, we were all taken in, and it's rare I don't go back to that night when I hear "I Want to Hold Your Hand." I can still see my mom just shaking her head when she saw those long-haired rockers from England.

"Maggie May" still brings me back to my basement, lying awake with my first clock radio tuned to a rock station. I got the radio for Christmas, and things were never the same. I had music at my disposal 24-7. I loved waking up at two in the morning to Rod Stewart and his amazing voice.

My house was sometimes filled with tunes from the Tijuana Brass, and I still love those upbeat, jazzy notes that were popular in the 1960s. Of course, commercials were always filled with cute, little jingles that you couldn't get out of your head. Remember "I'd Like to Buy the World a Coke"?

What would our life be like without music? It's a universal language, as Henry W. Longfellow wrote. Music brings us together and has the ability to take us back to days of our youth all the way until our old age. It's very hard to believe how many countless lyrics that are stashed in my brain, just waiting to be heard.

On the other hand, what would our lives be like with more stillness and solitude? I am amazed at the number of people, youth in particular, who never have a moment's silence. It seems so foreign to them. The millennial parents of today have begun to think there is something wrong in their lives if every minute is not scheduled or filled up with noise. Every room in the home is now equipped with a television. Super-surround sounds are installed in new houses, and the noise continues and gets louder and louder.

I have always found abundant peace when I return at the end of a workday and can just sit for a few minutes with complete silence. I find comfort in those times, and it is then that I have become closer to God and my mind opens up to what He is whispering to me.

> *Amazing grace! (how sweet the sound)*
> *That sav'd a wretch like me!*
> *I once was lost, but now am found,*
> *Was blind, but now I see.*
> *'Twas grace that taught my heart to fear,*
> *And grace my fears reliev'd;*
> *How precious did that grace appear,*
> *The hour I first believ'd!*

Thro' many dangers, toils and snares,
I have already come;
'Tis grace has brought me safe thus far,
And grace will lead me home.

—John Newton (1725–1807)

John Newton composed this song in 1779. Although he'd had some early religious instruction from his mother, who had died when he was a child, he had long since given up any religious convictions. However, on a homeward voyage, while he was attempting to steer the ship through a violent storm, he experienced what he was to refer to later as his "great deliverance." He recorded in his journal that, when all seemed lost and the ship would surely sink, he exclaimed, "Lord, have mercy upon us." Later in his cabin, he reflected on what he had said and began to believe that God had addressed him through the storm and that grace had begun to work for him.[3]

Mercy and grace go hand in hand, but first, we as Christians need to believe in the Lord and trust His forgiveness of our sins and the resurrection of our souls. In the second verse of this famous song, how does the grace of the Lord teach us to fear Him?

I believe the Lord's grace not only shows up in the amazing things that happen to us but also in the trials and tribulations that we have to witness as well. How can we know greatness without first knowing hurt and pain? Do we feel closer to God and His amazing grace when we are in need of a healing or helping hand? God would like us to witness and appreciate His great works in our everyday life and be gracious to Him equally so when we are granted His blessings.

---

[3] http://www.anointedlinks.com/amazing_grace.html

We can make our plans, but the Lord determines our steps.

Notes

Notes

Chapter 10

Sovereign Grace

October

For God sent not his Son into the world to condemn the world; but that the world through him might be saved.

—John 3:17

Many volumes have been written about God's sovereign grace, but do we understand the meaning of this word? Sovereignty in Webster's dictionary is described as the full right and power of a governing body to govern itself without any interference from outside sources or bodies. Sovereignty existed during the medieval period as the rights of nobility and royalty, the capability of individuals to make their own choices in life. God gives His sovereign grace without any help from us and gives it freely to all people, even nonbelievers. Examples of His sovereign grace are all around us.

This means He isn't coming to just tell us we are sinners, but He is coming to offer us His sovereign grace and forgiveness. When bad things happen to us, we can rely on the good things that

God has done for us entirely on His own. When the twin towers were destroyed, the Boston Marathon was bombed, or someone died in a car accident, did we at that time wonder why it happened to some people and not others?

We have all sinned numerous times or fallen short, or we may or may not be worse sinners than those who have died sudden and horrible deaths, but one thing is for sure. God does not determine how we live or die here on earth; He grants His grace to make sure we have eternal life after death. When we come close to death and are still around to talk about it, we often reflect on that experience and begin to question why we weren't chosen at that time or why God spared us in that moment.

When I was around ten or eleven, a tornado swept through our farmyard just after dark. It was a terrifying time for my mother and her six children who were left alone while the wind ripped through our property. We did not have a basement, so we remained in the house, trying to hold on just to survive. The next morning we went out to assess the damages and realized how fortunate we actually were. Our unattached garage was flattened, lying a mere hundred yards from our small farmhouse. The beautiful, big, red barn complete with a haymow on top that served dual purposes for our livestock was tore apart, and sticks were found a mile away.

I have gone back to that night many times and wondered why our lives were spared. It was nothing short of a miracle that our house was not in the path the storm took. If it were, none of us would have had a chance to survive. God's grace surrounded us, and I like to think the experience enhanced our lives. Out of tragedy came goodness, the same way it does when a crisis occurs and many people lose their lives.

Images of Grace

Those worn-out photos sitting in those old shoeboxes are just waiting for someone to study their faces and take a glimpse of sweet places of their past. The first thing we all start to go through when someone leaves us after a long life of trials and sacrifices is his or her photo albums. Years of history and nostalgia can be found between the pages. These can be pictures that bring history to life right before our eyes. Many times it is not faces we notice, but the color of the walls in their houses, the curtains, and the backgrounds that give us detail as well.

From the days of flashbulbs to instamatic to cell phones, we have certainly created a world of photos. Old black-and-whites are my favorites, telling of a time when people had values about the treasury of things that didn't come as easily as it does now. Photos taken at the click of a button, to delete or keep on a whim, is the norm today. Cell phones with data storage of unimaginable capability can capture our good times as well as our bad. We are not hesitant to simply delete the ones we don't like or will show hardship that makes our lives look unbalanced. Sharing on the Internet is the normal thing to do when we want the outside world to think our lives are rich and full. However, many people in this world do not live near relatives, and computers can keep families connected with photos in the blink of an eye. This has enriched many lives in this digital age.

But this generation is not even printing out their pictures for all of their close family members to look at. They are often made aware, if their phone is lost or their data is not retrievable, they have forfeited more than just their precious communication device. Fear sets in, and they have stress about it. Their intentions are good, but they never seem to get around to taking the pictures off their phones and putting them in an album. Oftentimes it is too late, and the regret can last for years.

When we were little and when my children were young, they would spend hours and hours sifting through Grandma's and Grandpa's photo albums. Many conversations were started around these picture books. Granted, the image quality of the pictures were jeopardized by the methods used to paste them in the books or put the clear plastic over them, but I think it was worth all of that just to see the looks on my children's faces as they stared at photos of me when I was young. This always raised questions in their minds and promoted conversation between generations.

Our memories can be a quiet calm in a sudden storm. They can bring to us a quiet stillness to a mind that is homesick or peace to an aging, lonely person who can look at a physical picture of his or her loved ones and go back home again. Let's bring back the age of photos, whether put on paper in a digital book or at the very least in an old box with a ribbon around them for times we just want to reminisce.

God's love and grace is sovereign. He has total control over all things past, present, and future. He gave us the ability to remember in our minds the beauty of the past and to be able to learn from our ancestors.

I do not understand the mystery of Grace;
Only that it meets us where we are.
But does not leave us where it found us.

—Anne Lamott

Notes

Notes

Chapter 11

Saying Grace

November

Give thanks to the Lord for he is good, his mercy endures forever.
—Psalm 107:1

My Grandmother's Table

This story has yet to be told to many members of my family, but in my opinion it bears telling. As my grandmother told me before she passed away, my maternal grandfather owned a dining room table that his own mother had possessed. I am guessing at the very least it is a hundred years old. It is a gorgeous, round, honey oak piece, solid and sturdy with three leaves that could be used to extend it to seat up to about twelve people. My aunt used it for a number of years, and then one weekend, her family, including four small children, packed up and moved out of town for severe financial reasons. They actually left in the middle of the night.

My wonderful, caring, prideful, and honest grandfather was

walking downtown later that same month and noticed a bank auction sign posted on a bulletin board. His beloved table was listed, and the sale was going to be heard in a few short days. As a small town, the bankers knew everyone, so my humble grandfather walked into this bank and proceeded to convince them not to sell the table. He even offered to pay something to get it back. He was so afraid to take a chance that someone would outbid him and he would never see his prized possession again. Times were tough, and he knew his bid would more than likely not be nearly high enough.

The kind banker, under no certain terms, told my grandfather to take the table and go on home. Many years have I sat at that table in their home, and it has become a true treasure to me. No price tag could be put upon its value to me. I feel so privileged to use this beautiful antique in my home today. My grandma gave it to me after my grandpa died. She had gone to live in an assisted living facility where she simply did not have room for it. I think her sentiment for that table was as strong as mine is today. She shared my grandpa's desire for me to have it because he knew I would take good care of it. Now I have the task of deciding which one of my children or grandchildren I will feel can carry on the legacy that was left to me. This decision will not be taken lightly, as I have shared this amazing story with my children.

One day a few years ago, I wrote the following poem to reflect my admiration for this beautiful heirloom.

Could They Imagine?
Sitting around my Grandma's round oak
table on a beautiful winter morning,

it's the one thing that has stayed the same and
never changed in over a hundred years,
built with love and gathered around by friends
and large families, in good times and bad,
having very little on their plates most of the
time or an overabundance in other years,
could they have ever imagined that this brisk, sunny, snowy
day my laptop sits atop the same round, oak table?
I am communicating with my son halfway
across the world as a marine overseas,
a country my great-grandparents were uncertain of,
all of their hopes, dreams, and ambitions lying out before them.
Many friends played numerous, rousing games of cards at
this table, ate delicious pies and desserts, and shared stories
of heartbreak, good fortune, and many grandchildren.
I will always feel quite small and humbled by their
stamina, their perseverance, and their love
of their family when I sit across this round, oak table.

The Apron

Aprons are not worn very often today, but you rarely, if ever, saw your grandmother without one while she was in the kitchen. I believe they wore them for a purpose, not a fashion statement, but in my opinion, they are works of art. They were also used to carry in eggs, gather vegetables, dust furniture, or wipe away tears from a crying child. Clothing was too hard to come by to get ruined by a spill in the kitchen, so garments were protected, if they could.

Pilgrim women wore mostly long, white ones. Waist aprons

were the norm after that, because cloth was scarce and times were tough. The bib apron usually was tied or buttoned in the back and served to safeguard their entire outfit.

In some quilt shops, apron patterns are making a comeback, and you can purchase one to make for both mother and daughter. Men are now wearing aprons while they are out grilling or cooking favorite meals at home.

In the late sixties and early seventies, a wedding reception involved young girls of the family chosen to be waitresses, and sewing them simple, lace aprons were a necessity. These vintage aprons can be seen in some antique stores now and bring me back to that special time.

Those gingham aprons started out pretty plain, but grandmas around the country later began to get fancier, and lace was more readily available, so more and more the women sewed their aprons with great pride as they impressed neighbor ladies at their social gatherings.

Old photos of women in the kitchen are rare without an apron displaying their talents, not only by the oven but as a seamstress too.

Saying Grace

Saying grace before a meal is a tradition that many Christians still continue practicing. In some American Christian families, either the head of the household or an honored guest often recites a special grace while the others observe a moment of silence. In some households it is customary for all at the table to hold hands during the grace. The following are variations of grace performed by different religions of the world:

- God is great. God is good. Let us thank him for our food. Amen.
- Come, Lord Jesus. Be our guest. Let this food of ours be blessed. Amen.
- Bless us, O Lord, and these thy gifts, which we are about to receive from Thy bounty through Christ our Lord. Amen.
- Be present at our table, Lord. Be here and everywhere adored.
- These mercies bless and grant that we may feast in fellowship with Thee. Amen.

> *I am grateful for what I am and have.*
> *My thanksgiving is perpetual.*
> —Henry David Thoreau.

God gave us eyes to see the beauty in nature, and
the Hearts to see the beauty in each other.

Notes

Notes

Chapter 12

In Your Good Graces

December

Let us then with confidence draw near to the throne of grace, that we may receive mercy and find grace to help in time of need.

—Hebrews 4:16

If we get in someone's good graces, we obtain a good opinion of ourselves from him or her. It makes us feel more accepted and loved. We often put too much emphasis on others' opinions and sometimes change ourselves to make sure that happens. We don't need to try to get into God's good graces. We are already there. So by doing more with your life or being more successful, generous, or gracious, that does not guarantee we will be more in God's good graces than anyone else.

The Seat Next to Me

Our airline seats were three rows apart on the return flight as my son and I boarded the plane toward home after a long weekend trip spent in San Diego. It was his first glimpse of the beautiful, blue Pacific Ocean, and I was so pleased to be able to offer my sixteen-year-old that special opportunity. We had seats right next to each other on the flight out on Friday night. As the plane took off, I could feel his excitement and apprehension, and I hoped we both would try to enjoy it without the cloud we had hanging over us from the events of the past year.

The trip was intended to be a family vacation, but my marriage had ended before we took the long, promised journey all together. My son and I were left to sort it all out. We enjoyed the beach, the shoreline, the weather, and the unfamiliar sights of Mexico. Our close friends welcomed us warmly, and our wounds began to heal a little bit as we spent days and nights in the glory of California, far away from our small town in the Midwest.

So as I took my seat on our layover flight home from Dallas, I was feeling quite satisfied at the events of the weekend. My mind and body, however, could not ever imagine how I could possibly live alone and be happy or find that peace I so longed for. I was fifty years old and facing a life ahead of me that I had never thought would happen. This was such an unfamiliar feeling that caught me off guard.

I looked up just as the elderly gentleman started coming up the aisle. He found his seat right next to me, gave me a little nudge on the shoulder, and declared, "Did you see that flight attendant?

It wouldn't kill her to smile at least! I don't know how she keeps her job."

I thought immediately, *I'm going to like this guy.*

He had a WWII veteran's cap on his head and seemed interested in talking to me so we started the usual way: Where are you from, what do you do, and where are you headed?

I asked him, "Where are you going?"

He replied, "My friend told me I could come and stay with her anytime I wanted to, so I decided to take her up on it."

He also proceeded to tell me about his previous relationships with women, and I was intrigued.

He said, "My first wife decided she liked the neighbor more than she liked me."

I became more interested and said, "I'm sorry to hear that."

"Don't be. I'm better off ... My second wife was a real gem. We bought a motor home together and traveled all over the United States. She ended up getting cancer and dying a few years back. I sure do miss her. But life goes on," he told me without hesitation.

I told him, "My marriage ended after thirty years, and my son is sitting a few rows back. We're on a family trip together."

We also talked about the war, and he started to say things but then would stop midsentence. While I listened and learned so much about wartime, it felt like time just flew by and we were landing soon.

He finally told me, if I wanted to truly learn about the war and what exactly happened during that time, I was to read a book he recommended "Absolute War by Chris Bellamy". As I kept talking to him, I started to realize one important fact. Life really does move forward. And if this man still knew how to love and enjoy women and live his life with joy after all he had been through, maybe my mere fifty years of life was far from being over. I know without a doubt that God gave me that seat next to him on that very day that I needed it the most.

When the plane landed, my son came up behind us.

The man spoke to him, "Is that your mom right here?"

And my son replied, "Yes, it is."

The kind WWII veteran who showed me so much in such a short amount of time stated simply, "You're so lucky!"

I only regret that I did not get that man's name and phone number, as I would love to be able to call him and tell him about my son, now a United States Marine, and how he gave me hope when I had very little left within my heart.

Notes

Notes

Chapter 13

Finding Grace

Just recently I have truly discovered the grace that I felt was missing throughout my life, hidden among the thorns and thistles that tore at my soul. I pursued writing a journal about my life experiences, all the while peering through the fogginess, eventually revealing the light of God's grace that He had granted to me without fail the moment I was born. God's grace and gifts are one in the same. Learning how to use those gifts from Him to ease each other's burdens are the very gifts of grace He was talking about in the Bible. "As every man hath received the gift, even so minister the same one to another, as good stewards of the manifold grace of God."

(1 Pet. 4:10).

From the time I was little as the fourth child raised in an abusive household, to a mother at twenty-four, to a recent divorcee who relocated, and finally to the woman I have become today, the wonderful grace of God has always been available to me. I believe it is also here for others who have gone through or are enduring life's inevitable struggles and tribulations. We can find God's grace through our friendships, families, or coworkers or just by looking at this awe-inspiring world He has made for us. It is how we use this grace to help ourselves and others that enables us to shed the prickly thorns that are woven throughout our minds and our physical bodies. This does not happen overnight in most cases, but it can be a daily journey and a spiritual walk with God that I slowly found myself willing to take.

My life now has become all the richer and all the more full of loveliness and meaning; much more enhanced by the way my eyes view it all. By mending broken relationships, seeking forgiveness from others, giving out forgiveness to my enemies, or just daily providing the same grace to others that I have been given, this year has been a reflection of all that I have been pursuing.

Timeline.
Nov 19, 2014 12:10pm
Laugh Lines

Lisa Droz
November 13, 2014

How much laughter did you actually hear today? Or how much did you laugh in the last week? Enough to transform that face of your youth into a map of laugh lines that can be traced all the way back to your childhood? How much of that laughter was yours alone, coming from somewhere inside of you?

God gave us a mouth to smile on the outside with, but along with that he gave us the gift of laughter that can follow it up. He also gave us a mind to develop a sense of humor-that great sense of humor we all need to have in order to face even the worst of our days. Some people seem to have a natural ability to make people laugh and others have to work at it a little harder. It can be developed and treasured by many around us.

Sometime ago, after years of searching for happiness, peace and a love of life; I found true joy and love and one day I discovered from somewhere within me a deep, throaty, full-bore laughter. Out it came all by itself without the least bit of effort. It came from a place inside of me that I didn't even know existed. It caught me off-guard. After all, I was well past my 50's when this happened. When I revealed that I had never laughed like that before in my whole life, the response I got was "Well, that is really sad". Immediately, my Grandma's words echoed in my mind. "Find someone that makes you laugh. Life is full of 1000's of reasons to make you cry."

There is a profound difference in our laughter-that gift that God gave to us. I am not referring to the sounds of laughter that distinguish us from one another. It's the ones from inside of us we can give to the world around us freely and with pure emotion or the half-hearted false ones meant to appease someone that some people carry around for years.

As toddlers, we laugh with our hearts open, unrestricted and energetic. Who hasn't heard a child's gut-laugh and been transformed? Then as we start to enter puberty, some girls develop that fake, flirty, giggly laugh that adolescent boys devour, thinking, "She must love me, I can always make her laugh."

We, as adults, are surrounded by laughter in our daily lives. Comic strips, advertising, magazines and even books can get us to laugh, but usually just on the inside. We pay money to see comedians all with the goal to get us to laugh.

Sadly, our time is spent on our phones, resorting to LOL or ROFL in the texting world, to at least let our friends know we have found their comment funny, for the moment. Anyone can get us to laugh at other people's misfortunes or mistakes or the crude or inappropriate humor that fills up our spaces. For a person to exhibit that Great humor that was intended for us they must be intelligent and interested in the world around us. Their humor is not driven by the need to laugh in the face of others but to make other people laugh with us. As for me, I'm rejoicing in my newfound laugh lines around my eyes and my smile as I know they are coming from a place within me that sat dormant for far too long. Humor is the best way to face our world today and in the future.

Notes

Notes

About the Author

Lisa Marie is a newly published author. She lives in Rapid City, South Dakota, and is a graduate of WDT Institute with a degree in library media. Lisa is currently working for the RCCSS in the library field.

She enjoys reading, hiking, photography, writing, and sharing her thoughts about current issues. She is a tour guide in the summer months in the heart of the beautiful Black Hills of South Dakota. With God's help, she has overcome financial diversity, divorce, and relocation, and she puts her Christian faith as an important part of her life. Follow her and her writing on her blog www.anoutsidelook.livejournal.com.

Made in the USA
Columbia, SC
12 April 2021

35969209R00069